SAGITTARIUS

31 Days of Soul

A Mini-Series
Poetry Collection

By Tristiny Bell

SAGITTARIUS
31 Days of Soul

A Mini-Series
Poetry Collection

From the author of
Aquarius: A 28 Day Journey

By Tristiny Bell

To the fiery passionate being who looks at the world as their playground. May your spirit continue to be blessed with the eternal flower of life

Contents

Day 1 - All the Above

Choosing is easy.
Deciding is hard.
Today, I chose.
It's the right choice,
But the wrong decision.

We decide but then…
We are wrong.

So, what's really right?
Is it just wrong for now?

To be or Not to be?
We chose to be.
I chose to be.

For a decision that was never ours
But we still choose every hour

Judge shall we not
But judge is how we do

My mistake today but
tomorrow it's on you

TRISTINY BELL

Day 2 - 8th Inning

Back at it again
Call it the 68th time
Here's another win
Or maybe a tie
Bases are loaded
Let's give it a try

Strikeeee one
Should've stayed even
But this game isn't done
Took a last sip of water,
Stepped up to the plate
Positioned to conquer
Tighten up the grip
Just to swing a bit harder

Strikeeee two
Too early to forfeit
Choke up, choke up
Forget about the pit
But the cheers stop
And all wait in silent
For this next swing
We'll need guidance

Day 3 - Self Isolate

Confined to these walls
Contained in thought
Captured by them all
Contagious enough
Continued to spread
Caught up in despair
Crippling each leg
Crossed minds instead

Washing away more than sin
Our cleanse will now begin

Day 4 - Caught Up

Ropes and chains
Guess we're still tied up.
Leather and belts
Let the knocks interrupt
Or don't. We love noise
And sounds, we erupt.
This ain't for the boys
But the men, we fuck
Fuck up that is
And kids come rush
Out the blue from lust

Now here we are again
Back in the chains
From our own demise
That was never the plan
Our souls compromised

Day 5 - Another Storm

Roll of thunder but I don't cry
The air turns thick and heavy
While the birds flee the sky
Lightning chases the clouds
As it moves from dusk to dawn
Waking up to the chaos
The perfect alarm

Day 6 - Kinfolk

I am not my hair, but my hair is me
Locs flowing down to the knee
Maybe not yet but soon you'll see
A tangled web of her story
Combing through the mystery
Finding our own controversy

My neck, my back
Thirty inches down to my crack
It's not the image that I lack
Just the soul you forget
That'll make you soon regret
EVERYONE! quiet on the set!

Because y'all not hearin'
This queen here sparin'
No feelings. I feel you fearin'
The rapture of the present
Tho my presence not a present
Or you'll fall like a peasant

No simple person, place, or thing
So, I'm not that chick from mainstream
But when I speak, these Bells sing
Hallelujah. Praise Him Amen
We may not be family but we Kin
Folks skin. We'll be back again

12

Day 7 - Which Love

Who do you run to when you need love?
Not a want, a desire, or a lust
but a need for all the above?

Or a family love that's strong enough
To give you all the comfort needed—
Even when you are wrong

Maybe a friend love full of concern.
Jokes and laughs might get it done.
Or, is it fiery passion you yearn?

From a friendly friend you desire
But that love is a forbidden love
And, your soul still feels the fire

What's left is an eternal flame
That burns within, around the clock
Giving all the love for every pain
It's a love that needs nothing else
Just a love with nothing to gain

Day 8 - Numb

A clean slate, a clean start
Not the memories
Just moments of dark

Nothing. Nothing in heart
No laughs or cries
But a rock, solid hard

Nothing is also art
There's more there
It's just deep in the dark

It's no mystery in disguise
Just secrets and known lies

Day 9 - Here Now

Screeching yet again
Every twelve minutes it's a reminder
That you're finally here.
Here— where your heart is
Was
Where your heart was
But you're finally here

Damn another flashback
Scrolling through time; now you're gone
But you're somehow still there
There— where your heart was
Is
Where your heart still is
But you're finally gone

Day 10 - Never Too Much

A kiss…. just to feel you
Wrapped in your spell
Our souls heal you
Then the real unveils

A hundred thoughts
Of how if should be
Hoping to adjust to
The visions so vividly

A thousand hugs
Emerged in your touch
Trapped by those arms
This moment we rush

A million days
Submerged in your heart,
Giving you my all
Right from the start

Never too much
Never too much

Day 11 - Up Late Again

Alarm is set.
Lights are off.
Now for a little white noise.
Wait— I've never seen this.
Thirty minutes go by...
Time for a second try.

This time with eyes shut.
Did I clear the counter?
What time is that meeting?
Remember that one tweet—
Nope, nope, not again.

Phone, faced down, far away.
It's pitch black, silent, quiet.
Maybe I should do some work
I can't believe she said that
Was that really his first na—

I give in.
You up?

Day 12 - Brown Skin Girl

First, it's your skin that spikes fear
Golden hues of purple
Can even turn a pale one blue

Deepened and true
Stern in your move

You are enough.

Then, it's the hair they despise
Locs to curls to fros
Rooted in magic and stories

Free as the mind
Knitted in passion

You are enough.

Now, our voices are too known.
They call it loud or anger but
We know it was never the tone.

They will hear us
They will see us

You are enough.
Brown skinned girl.

Day 13 - ICU

Write. Delete. Repeat.
It's a never-ending circle
But this needs a break
So now I see.
Turn it to the side
Now it's for you
Take away the curve
For a pair of eyes

Day 14 - Clouded

Even clouded judgment
Knows the real reality
No dream or wish
Could create that fallacy

Inhale lies, exhale truth
Ashing the bullshit
Roll another for just you

Day 15 - I Love You

I love you from toenail to tooth
From your favorite hats
To those damn cowboy boots.
Even miles away I feel your truth

I love how you question it all.
Standing up for others
But they'll never let you fall.
For peace, you love a good brawl.

They're rooting for everyone black.
Just know I'm cheering for you.

Day 16 - More

It's always more
More money, more problems
It's always more
But I want more too
More love
More joy
More life

To the point it looks different
What is this word we desire…
More
More, more, more, more,
After a while, it looks unfamiliar
More
More
M O R E
Seeking and seeking
For what we soon forget
Soon can't recognize
Soon for not needed

More of future past desires
Consumed before us now.

Day 17 - Karma

Karma's a bitch, right?
At least…
That's word on the street
But who is Karma?
Is it she or he?
Person, place or thing?
Either way,
Can't wait for y'all to meet.

Or, is it that time
You tried to get by?

Or, maybe last year
When you told that one lie?

Is it all the people
You've wronged over time?

It could be from
The day you skipped line.

Just know it's
A force with no sense of time.

Day 18 - Where

This feels like last year
I remember this feeling
Same sound
Same energy
Same feelings
This all too familiar

But there's one difference
Same who
Same what
Same when

But the where
The difference is in
The where

36

Day 19 - Cussed

Fuck!
Oh, that's right
We can't curse huh
Well, go to hell
Damn that's another one

You've cursed my blood
And now I gotta hush
Breaking habits you passed
But one lil' word makes you blush

Or angry maybe
Because I wouldn't know
Emptiness is hidden within
But it's a smile you show

We just want to break free
And feel like we're alive
But this some hard ass shit
Damn now that's five

Wait, I just lied
So here goes lucky number seven:
We bust our ass everyday
Just to make it to heaven

Day 20 - Gone

How can you feel everything
And still end up speechless?
How do you feel these thoughts?
Still silent. No voice.
Except mine inside.
It's quiet this time.
What happened
To candid women
With hearts of gold
And speech of steel?
What happened to her?

Day 21 - Circle of Life

When we first met, we crawled
Then we walked.
Next, we ran.
We jumped, then we flew.
And now we're dead.

Day 22 - I Had a Dream

Was it a dream?
I'm awake now
But those moments…

Were they make believe?
Did I let my imagination
Run, leap, and jump?

Was it even real?
Because now all I have
Are the memories.

Is it all in my head?
I have no proof
Except the way I feel.

Did we truly exist?
All I have to show
Are the memories.

But now I close my eyes,
Praying for that dream.
I get blanks.
I try harder and harder
Squeezing my eyes tighter.

Dreams like that only come once.
Now, I close my eyes each day,
Wishing that dream will come back.

Day 23 - Your Side of the Bed

Firm, cold, and untouched
It was missing your skin
But your scent left much

Just enough to remind me
That you're away now,
But here all the time.

Not twenty-four-seven,
But three hundred
And sixty dimes.

Add five more to see why
We've multiplied by nine
To get one of a kind.

Day 24 - Do You Remember?

You came in with power
Head high and strong
And a pleasing smile
The energy shifted
I looked at you different
From everyone in the room
Because for me,
It was just you
Subconsciously observing
Your gesture, your soul
Back then I didn't know
But now I'm in a hold

Day 25 - Untitled

Screams aren't enough but somehow
Yelling is a little too much.
When we raise our voices,
You start to get a bit rough.
So, we speak on playing fields
Just to get passed over

History may repeat itself but
Only a fool gets burned twice

Day 26 - Drugged Up

Addicted to familiar love
That you've been here before
And you know where to go
Or even how fast or slow

Addicted to familiar love
Where the softest touch
Leads to the firmest caress,
Giving a hell of a rush

Addicted to familiar love
Not the being or even flesh
But the way my soul remembers
Every emotion it felt

Addicted to familiar love
With the hills and the valleys
When you mix it all together
Still wondering what happened

Addicted to familiar love
Somehow my drug of choice
Ask me to quit but I'm
Ready for a double dose

52

Day 27 - Confession

Dear diary,

I have a confession.
But to confess is to lie
Or to have lied.
Lied to one's self.
So, let me rectify.
My bravery is false.
Because even I'm terrified
Of what's next,
What happened
And what I am.
Who I am,
Where I am
Now that's off my chest
I have more to confess.
One deep breath
I need God for this one
He'll tell you the rest.

Day 28 - If I Was a Bird

Soaring the night sky for answers
To all the questions within

Finding eternal peace with just
The wind beneath my wings

Admiring all the stars above
From dusk to dawn

Absorbing evaporated energies
With each breath taken

Never looking to the earth.
For my journey is elsewhere

Day 29 - Please

Never have to beg for it
But this time…
When I say please, I need you deep.
Penetrate every insecurity you read.
I don't even want to feel what's true.
Only the pressure you came to release.

Last time you hurt me
But this time I'm ready.
Touch me gently first, for a little tease
Unfortunately, you're in for a treat.
I came prepared for your troubles.
Don't stop there. Get on your knees.

58

Day 30 - God's Calling

He told me I was so close
So close that I can feel it
His energy, his existence
I can hear his voice louder

Closed eyes, heads bowed
Walking blind in full vision
Leading by faith, not ego
My soul in full surrender

My spirit is being called
Putting my body in auto
So, here I am awakened
Coming to you, on my way.

Day 31 - Real World *Bonus*

Sticks and stones may break my bones
but words will never hurt...
So they say
With sharpened daggers
And flying bullets of hate
How much is she really supposed to take?
Back to the ponytails and pin curls
Baby girl got a taste of the real world.
So trusting, so sweet
That friendly face forced his place into her space.
But it's okay, huh?
'Cause it was all at a slow pace.
Confused.
Baby girl had no clue what to do.
See, they didn't address this at elementary school.
Baby just entered the real world,
Where her youth plays no factor,
As her soul feels the rapture.
Yet her virtue doesn't even matter
To this man,
Who was only stopped by a small bladder.
Stopped by a small bladder.
Not because it was an awful thing to do
Or because she trusted you.
No.
Because baby girl had to use the restroom.
Welcome to the real world, huh.
Where no one gives a damn about who you are
Or where you come from.
I don't mean to sound rude.
Early on I learned the truth
From the BS to finesse

And the negative comments some express,
To the ignorance people tend to possess
And the lack of respect to characters they neglect.
Welcome to the real world.

SAGITTARIUS

www.ingramcontent.com/pod-product-compliance
Lightning Source LLC
Chambersburg PA
CBHW021341160726
47994CB00007B/2803